CREATIVE CRAFTS FOR ALL SEASONS

projects that help kids learn

CREATIVE CRAFTS FOR ALL SEASONS

projects that help kids learn

Anne Campbell
Kathryn Waite
Anne Mikelonis

RCL

Allen, Texas

Send all inquiries to:
RCL • Resources for Christian Living
200 East Bethany Drive
Allen, Texas 75002-3804

Telephone: 877-275-4725
Fax: 800-688-8356

Visit us at **www.rclweb.com**
Customer Service E-mail: **cservice@rcl-enterprises.com**

Printed in the United States of America

Library of Congress Number 99-75186

21113   ISBN 0-7829-0091-4

5 6 7 8 9 10 11 12 13
07 08 09 10 11 12 13

CONTENTS

Introduction 7

Part I: Sacraments

Painted Votive Candleholder 12
Holy Water Font 14
First Communion Banner 16
We Are Jesus' Sheep 18
Fragrant Anointing Oil 20
Vocation Collage 21
Altar Cloth and Stole 22
Gifts of the Holy Spirit Mobile 24

Part II: Scripture

Creation Mural 28
Israelite City Preparing for Passover 30
Stories of Healing Fabric Banner 32
Clay Cross of Forgiveness 34
Sand Paint Fish 36
Mosaic Rainbow 37
Fish Trivet 38
Pentecost Bookmark 40
The Armor of God 42
God is My Rock 44

Part III: Seasons

Advent Dough Wreath 46
"I Am God's Precious Gift" Ornament 48
Jesse Tree 50
Christmas Altarpieces 52
Holy Family Triarama 54
Epiphany Card 56
Lent to Easter Flower 58
Hot Cross Buns 60
Stations of the Cross 61
Easter Lily Card 62

Part IV: Saints

Holy Card Magnets 66
Stick Puppet Saint 68
Our Lady of Guadalupe Mosaic 70
Life of Mary Banner 72
Patron Saint Placemat 74
Puppet Theater and More Puppet Ideas 76

Part V: Prayers

The Rosary 80
Personal God Box 82
Prayer Pal 84
Guardian Angel 86
Spiritual Bouquet 90
Crayon Resist Creed 92
Praying Hands 95

INTRODUCTION

Being creative with arts and crafts in catechetical sessions can be an enjoyable and memorable time for you and your children. In this book, we will offer many arts and crafts activities using a variety of mediums and techniques. Arts and crafts offer an opportunity to put the experience of faith into a concrete and tangible object.

Children are capable of taking ordinary objects and creating a new object of great meaning. Years ago, my seven-year-old son created a simple, meaningful craft in Vacation

Church School. On a good-sized, oval-shaped, smooth rock he painted the words "God is my rock," and colorfully decorated the rock. Eight years later, the rock is still at home in our garden. John's rock sits with other important family rocks and shells collected from our vacations across the country. When we look at the rock, we are reminded of God's continuing love, protection, and guidance in our lives.

Crafts can also be a way of service and outreach to others. A project made at a retreat or a day of reflection can serve as a reminder of that time. Craft activities can become a way to share a faith experience with senior citizens, preschool groups, and those in hospitals and nursing homes.

Begin by collecting materials to be creative! Your children are capable of making wonderful objects out of the ordinary. Give them the opportunity to explore, express, and create new and different ideas.

ITEMS TO COLLECT

In one box or tote, have available a supply of basic materials:

- crayons
- markers
- glue or glue sticks
- good scissors
- tape
- sharp pencils
- poster board
- construction paper
- drawing paper
- paper for finger paints

- finger paint
- tempera paint
- small sponges
- clothes pins
- dowel rods

- paper plates
- tooth picks
- popsicle sticks
- paint stirring sticks
- assorted paint brushes

Store food items such as rice, a variety of beans, and assorted shapes of pasta in airtight containers. Save buttons, cotton balls, clean and empty frozen juice cans, oatmeal containers, and egg cartons. Collect pieces of fabric (burlap, seasonal calicos, gingham, old solid sheets, drapery lining, denim). Pieces of rick-rack, lace, ribbon, felt, and yarn are great for trimming projects.

To protect the floor and tables, use plastic drop cloths, plastic table cloths, or tarps. Old shirts or art smocks are good cover-ups. Wax paper is a good placemat for smaller projects.

GETTING STARTED

This book is divided into five sections, each containing an assortment of projects. The craft ideas can be used in many flexible ways. For example, the Pentecost bookmark can be made as a gift for those preparing for the sacrament of Confirmation, as well as for personal use.

All good activities begin with a purpose and a goal. When choosing a craft, be certain the activity is tied to the lesson or liturgical season. Keep in mind the time that the children will spend on a given project, as well as their abilities to do the activity. Crafts should be a challenging experience, not a frustrating experience. If extra hands are needed, call upon parents or teens to assist. Have difficult cutting or assembly prepared ahead of time. Each child's personality and creativity will be expressed through his or her art. The catechist's role is to provide positive support for the children's efforts.

Use each craft project in this book as a springboard for your own new projects. Adapt the crafts to your own themes. Most of the projects are simple and can be done with easily obtained materials. Age guidelines are not given, so know the capabilities of your children and plan accordingly. You may want to make the craft before the children do to familiarize yourself with the process of assembly. Have all supplies ready to go at classtime. Relax and enjoy your arts and crafts!

PART I—SACRAMENTS

Signs and symbols that we can see, feel, and smell help us experience the sacraments. The craft projects presented in this section remind us that we are members of the body of Christ. Through sacraments, we experience God's love, his forgiveness, and the power of the Holy Spirit.

PAINTED VOTIVE CANDLEHOLDER

Topic: Initiation

The newly baptized are given a lighted candle as a sign that Jesus Christ, the light of the world, is with them. The lit candle reminds us to be the light of Christ to others. The completed project can be used as part of a group prayer service. (Adult supervision is necessary when using matches and burning candles.)

What You Need

- Clean, empty baby food jars
- Scraps of torn color tissue paper
- White glue diluted with water
- Paintbrush
- Clear enamel spray (optional)
- Fine-tip black marker
- Votive candle

Steps to Follow

1. Apply glue mixture on outside surface of jar.
2. Arrange tissue paper pieces on jar, allowing edges to overlap.
3. Use paintbrush with diluted glue to secure paper edges.
4. Allow glue and paper to dry.
5. Use a black marker to write on the dry paper to create a "stained glass."
6. Spray with clear enamel if desired.

HOLY WATER FONT

Topic: Baptism

Jesus began his public ministry by asking John the Baptist for baptism. Jesus received his Father's affirmation and took up the task he was sent to do. When we enter a church, we bless ourselves with holy water and recall our own baptism. This project extends this act into the child's home.

What You Need

- Wet clay (Crayola is recommended; one box will supply about 20 children.)
- Dull pencil
- Water

Steps to Follow

1. With wet clay, mold a font that can hold water. (Clay does not harden until placed in water, so children can mold and reshape their creations until they are satisfied with their work.)
2. Use a dull pencil to scratch religious symbols in the clay.
3. Poke a small hole in the top of the font.
4. Place the font in a dish of water for 4 to 6 hours.
5. Upon removal, wash the font in warm water and let it dry.
6. Hang and fill with water.

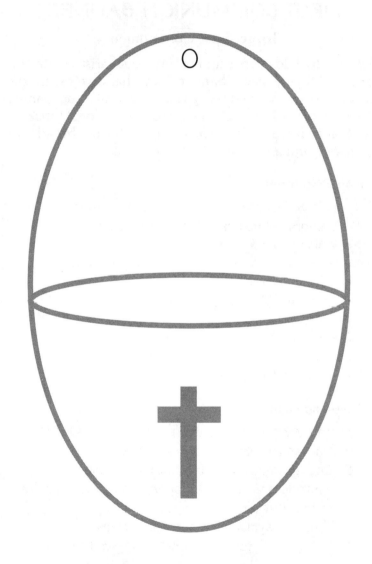

FIRST COMMUNION BANNER

Topic: First Communion

Have each child preparing for First Eucharist create this banner. Display each banner in a hallway or in the Church foyer. A great keepsake! Decorate the banner with symbols of Initiation: a lighted candle for Baptism, a cross for Reconciliation, a chalice and bread for Eucharist, and a dove for the Holy Spirit.

What You Need

- Felt in assorted colors (purple, tan, white, primary colors) cut into 6" × 5" pieces
- White felt 6½" × 30"
- Assorted colors of fabric paint (small tip)
- Wooden dowel, 7½" long
- Patterns of shapes cut from tagboard
- Craft Glue
- Scissors
- Pencil
- Yarn cut into 14" pieces

Steps to Follow

1. Fold over the top (width) of the white felt 1½". Sew at the hem to form a rod pocket.
2. Enlarge the tagboard patterns. Choose four symbols and trace the shapes on various colors of felt. Cut out the shapes.
3. Glue the symbols on the white banner.
4. Using fabric paint, decorate the symbols as

16

desired. Each child can write his (her) name and the date of his (her) First Communion on the banner.

5. Insert the dowel into the rod pocket. Tie yarn at each end of the dowel.

6. Dry flat overnight.

Additional symbols for First Communion Banner found with Gifts of the Holy Spirit Mobile and Clay Cross of Forgiveness projects.

WE ARE JESUS' SHEEP

Topic: Reconciliation

In the gospel of John, chapter 10, Jesus uses the image of the shepherd and the sheep as a sign of himself and his followers. He teaches us that he cares for us and protects us, and that we are his followers. When we stray, he will carefully redirect us. Children can make this sheep as they prepare for the sacrament of Reconciliation.

What You Need

- White poster board
- Cotton balls, torn and rolled into small pea-sized balls
- Fine-tip color markers
- Glue
- Scissors

Steps to Follow

1. Using the pattern (enlarged), cut out a sheep.
2. Glue the small pea-sized balls of cotton onto the body of the sheep.
3. Using markers, color the hooves and the face of the sheep.

Extension activity

Create a bulletin board of the sheep created by all of the children preparing for Reconciliation. On the background, draw an outline of Jesus and the words "Jesus is the Good Shepherd." Have each child write his (her) name on the sheep's leg.

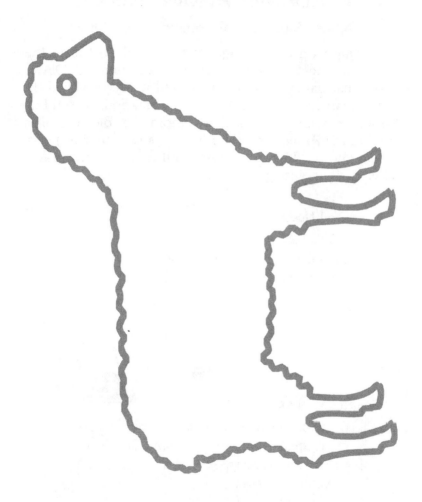

**Sheep pattern for We Are Jesus' Sheep Project and as
additional First Communion Banner symbol.**

FRAGRANT ANOINTING OIL

Topics: Baptism, Confirmation, Holy Orders

Anointing with oil is a sign of God's call to live in the Spirit. In the Old Testament, Samuel anointed David. From that day on, the Spirit of God was with David. In the sacraments of Baptism, Confirmation, and Holy Orders, chrism oil is used for anointing. Blessed oil is used in the Anointing of the Sick as a reminder of Jesus' healing power. Use this fragrant oil for your own prayer services of anointing.

What You Need

- Small empty vial or bottle
  (available at craft store or local pharmacy)
- Small funnel
- Olive oil
- Perfumes
- Eye dropper

Steps to Follow

1. Using the small funnel, have each child pour a small amount of olive oil in bottle.
2. Using the eye dropper, add a few drops of perfume in bottle.
3. Shake gently.

VOCATION COLLAGE

Topic: Holy Orders, Matrimony

The sacraments of Holy Orders and Matrimony enable us to serve in the Church. Invite the children to create a collage expressing the vocation of living out these sacraments at the Service of Communion. For Matrimony, look for pictures of family life such as eating, playing, and praying together. For Holy Orders, find pictures of aspects of ministry, such as leading worship, teaching, mission work, and other kinds of service to the Church.

What You Need

- Magazines
- Newspapers
- Glue
- Paper
- Markers
- Poster board
- Samples of sacramental symbols

Steps to Follow

1. Draw symbols on paper and cut out pictures related to one or both of the sacraments.
2. Arrange and glue on poster board.

ALTAR CLOTH AND STOLE

Topic: Eucharist

An altar cloth is used to cover the altar during the celebration of the Liturgy of the Eucharist. A stole is a narrow piece of cloth worn by men who are ordained. The priest wears his stole over both shoulders. Deacons wear stoles draped over their left shoulder. This project is a class or group project and can be created in preparation for First Communion, as an end-of-the-year project, at the close of a retreat or Vacation Church School, or to celebrate a special event.

What You Need
- Construction paper
- Bulletin board paper
- Markers
- Scissors
- Glue
- Pre-cut 6" squares of different colored construction paper

Steps to Follow
1. Measure the table top or altar. Add 12" to each side. For example, if the altar top measures 20" x 60", cut the bulletin board paper 44" x 84".
2. Cut 12" diagonal slits from each corner toward the center. This will allow the paper to drape down the sides.

3. Invite the children to trace their hands on a pre-cut square and write something for which they are thankful. Some children may want to decorate with sacramental symbols.
4. Glue completed squares along the border of the paper covering.

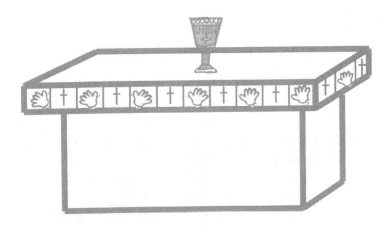

GIFTS OF THE HOLY SPIRIT MOBILE

Topic: Confirmation

The seven gifts of the Holy Spirit are wisdom, understanding, judgement, courage, knowledge, reverence and a sense of wonder and awe. Create this mobile to increase awareness of the Holy Spirit's presence and influence in our lives and in our community.

What You Need

- Styrofoam plate
- Heavy thread or lightweight string
- Variegated wrapping paper
    in red, yellow, or orange pattern
- Black marker or pen
- Pencil with sharp point
- Scissors

Steps to Follow

1. Enlarge dove pattern and trace on styrofoam plate. Cut out dove. Using a sharp pencil, poke holes in dove as shown on pattern.
2. Using flame pattern, trace on variegated paper and cut out seven flames.
3. Write one gift of the Holy Spirit on each flame, using a black marker or pen.
4. Using string, attach flames to dove. Tie string at middle hole to hang your mobile.

**Dove and Holy Spirit symbols to be used for
Gifts of the Holy Spirit Mobile and as additional
First Communion Banner symbol.**

PART II—SCRIPTURE

Children of all ages have favorite scripture stories. Craft projects enable children to visualize and remember these stories. A few favorite scripture stories and themes from the Old and New Testaments are offered in this section.

CREATION MURAL

Topic: Creation Story

Read Genesis 1:1–31 and/or Genesis 2:1–25. Each group or class is assigned the task of making items for a given day of creation. Make your mural as large or as small as desired. The larger mural looks great with many examples from each category. The size of the background pieces will determine the overall finished size. Use one large sheet of bulletin board paper as the background and add each groups' creation a "day" at a time. Use your imagination when creating!

What You Need

- Bulletin board paper
- Assorted colors of construction paper
- Glue, scissors
- Crayons or markers

Steps to Follow

1. Assign each group or class a specific day of creation.
2. Create the following, using construction paper, markers, glue, and scissors:

Day 1:	sky (both night and day)
Day 2:	seas and sky
Day 3:	dry land with plants
Day 4:	stars, moon, and sun
Day 5:	sea life and birds
Day 6:	living creatures, man and woman

3. Day six has many creatures, so you can assign some of these to other groups.
4. Assemble by gluing the sky to the background. Then add the items from each day in order. Some items may overlap; for example, the mountains may overlap the sky and the sea animals may overlap the water.

Extension Activity

Read the Genesis account as the mural is being assembled by the students. Display the mural in a hallway bulletin board.

ISRAELITE CITY
PREPARING FOR PASSOVER

Topic: Passover

The observance of Passover began in Egypt when God freed his people from slavery. Moses warned the pharaoh of the impending plagues if he did not free the Israelites. One night, many Egyptian children died in their homes. The Israelite children were spared. Finally, the pharaoh released the Israelites, and they passed from slavery to freedom.

What You Need

- Brown lunch bags
- Gray or brown construction paper
- Ruler
- Pencil
- Paper scraps
- Glue
- Newspapers
- Stapler
- Scissors
- Crayons

Steps to Follow

1. Using crayons or paper scraps, decorate the front of the paper bag to look like a stone house. For example, use the gray crayon to color stones for the walls; use brown for a wooden door and door posts on three sides. Make windows with shutters.

2. Cut the construction paper one inch wider than the width of the paper bag and fold in half. Use crayons to decorate the roof.

3. Open bag and stuff lightly with crumpled newspaper. Fold over top of sack about two inches and staple shut.

4. Place construction paper roof over top of sack and glue to attach.

5. Assemble village and review Passover story.

Option: Add people and attach to brown poster board to make a village. Use a red crayon to mark door posts.

STORIES OF HEALING
FABRIC BANNER

Topic: Scripture Themes of Healing,
Reconciliation, and Forgiveness

The scriptures have many accounts of Jesus healing people. The healing of a blind man (Mk. 8:22–25), the healing of Jairus' daughter (Mk. 5:21–24, 35–43), and the cure of a paralyzed man (Lk. 6:6–11) are a few examples from the gospels. Create this banner to illustrate a favorite story of healing, which will serve as a reminder to build our own faith in God's healing power.

What You Need

- Fabric crayons (Crayola works best.)
- Notebook paper (Ignore lines.)
- 2 Dowels, ¼" diameter x 10" or 12½" long
- Stapler
- Iron
- Newspaper
- White fabric cut into 14" x 10" pieces
- Yarn

Steps to Follow

1. Using fabric crayons, draw a picture illustrating a scripture account of Jesus healing someone. Do not use words, as the drawing will reverse upon printing.

2. Place fabric on newspaper and then place picture face down on fabric.
3. Using a warm, dry iron, transfer the picture to the fabric.
4. Then let fabric cool; trim any excess edges.
5. Use the glue to attach dowels to top and bottom of picture. Roll dowel once and staple back to secure.
6. Cut a piece of yarn and tie to top ends of dowel to hang.

CLAY CROSS OF FORGIVENESS

Topic: Sin

The symbol of the cross reminds us of the death and resurrection of Jesus. Jesus offers us forgiveness, and reminds us to forgive others (Luke 17:3).

What You Need

- Modeling clay
- Paper plates to work the clay on
- "U" shaped wire for hanger or a coat hanger, cut and bent to form a "U" shape
- Acrylic paints, paintbrush
- Clear Acrylic spray
- Rolling pin

Steps to Follow

1. Distribute clay and paper plates.
2. Enlarge cross patterns. With a lump of clay, roll clay flat to the desired thickness and cut out a cross using one of the cross patterns. Or, roll a small piece of clay to form "snakes," and twist or braid to form a cross.
3. Insert open ends of hanger at the top on back side of cross, being careful not to poke through to front of cross.
4. Lay flat to dry on the paper plate.
5. Paint as desired, and spray with a clear acrylic finish.

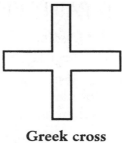

Greek cross

Latin cross

Celtic cross

SAND PAINT FISH

Topic: Discipleship

Jesus told the apostles to be fishers of men. The fish was a staple of life in the time of Jesus and a part of the miracle of the feeding of the multitudes. The fish became a sign of Christianity in the early Church.

What You Need

- Tagboard
- Colored sand, each color in a separate sealed container
- Pencil, Ruler
- Wax paper
- Glue, Scissors
- Small paintbrush
- Clean, small plastic container (empty margarine tub)

Steps to Follow

1. Cut out a fish shape from tagboard using the fish patterns (enlarged).
2. Using a pencil, draw sections on the fish, forming squares, rectangles, circles, and triangles.
3. Put a small amount of glue in the plastic container. Starting at the center of the fish, use the paintbrush to spread a small section of glue on fish.
4. Sprinkle the section with one color of sand. Repeat the process of glue and sand, creating a colorful design. Lay flat to dry on wax paper.
5. If the fish curls, lay another piece of wax paper on top and cover with a book until dry.

MOSAIC RAINBOW

Topic: God's Covenant with Noah (see Genesis 9:13)

What You Need

- Assorted dried beans: red, white, brown, and green; brown and white rice or colored rice (from craft store)
- 5" x 7" matting cutout scraps from a frame shop
- Glue, Pencil
- Paintbrush
- Small plastic containers

Steps to Follow

1. Using a pencil, outline a rainbow on the matting.
2. Pour a small amount of glue into the plastic container.
3. Paint a line of glue on the outline of the rainbow, and apply the rice/beans along the line of the rainbow.
4. Repeat glue and beans/rice.
5. Allow to dry flat.

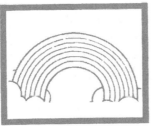

FISH TRIVET

Topic: Faith

A traditional symbol of our faith, the fish was used in a number of gospel stories. Jesus fed his followers in Luke 9:10–17 and called the apostles to be fishers of men in Mark 1:16–18. To the early Christians, the fish was a symbol of their faith. This craft requires some adult help in preparing the wood, but craft is easy to assemble.

What You Need

- Sandpaper
- Wood glue
- Wood shelving, ³⁄₄" thick
- Dowels, ¼" cut in two 6" pieces

Steps to Follow

1. Enlarge fish patterns to appropriate size for a trivet. Using pattern A as your guide, prepare the wood shapes for the children. With your assistance, children can complete steps 2 through 4. On the back side of fish, use a router to cut out two ¼" grooves the length of the fish along the broken lines. Cut fish into five pieces, as marked by the solid lines on pattern.
2. Sand all the cut edges of the wood pieces.
3. Lay the pieces on a covered work surface, grooved side up. Lay the dowel pieces lengthwise in the grooves. An extra piece of dowel can be used as a guide for spacing between the cut pieces of the fish.
4. Glue the pieces together (pattern B).

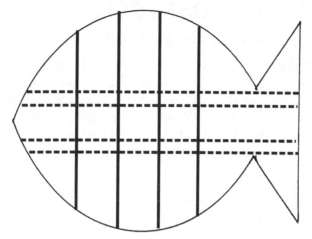

(A) Cutting and routing lines for fish trivet

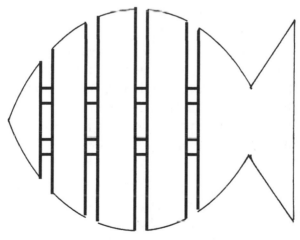

(B) Finished fish trivet

PENTECOST BOOKMARK

Topics: Pentecost, Confirmation

The power of the Holy Spirit is beyond words, and the scriptures use images to describe the effects of the Spirit of God. Empowered by the gift of the Holy Spirit, the apostles boldly proclaimed the gospel. The images described in Acts 2:1–11 are the basis for this craft activity.

What You Need

- Ribbon, 1½" to 2" wide, approx. 8" long
- Unlined index card, cut to approx. 2" x 5"
- Markers or color pencils
- Sharp scissors or exacto knife

Steps to Follow

1. Cut two slits the width of the ribbon, about ¾" down from each short edge of index card.
2. Decorate the card, using markers or color pencils, drawing symbols or images described in the Pentecost event. Children may want to draw a dove to represent the Holy Spirit.
3. Insert the ribbon through the slits, sliding it behind the drawing.

THE ARMOR OF GOD

Topic: God's Strength

In Ephesians 6:10–17, Paul advises Christ's followers to draw strength from God's power. Paul uses the imagery of protective armor to stand against evil.

What You Need

- Poster board
- Liquid starch, water
- Tempera paint or food coloring
- Paintbrushes, containers to hold paint
- Table salt

Steps to Follow

1. Cut poster board in half.
2. Mix together ⅛ cup liquid starch, ⅛ cup water, 1 Tbs. tempera or 2 drops of food coloring, and ½ cup table salt. Stir frequently. Repeat for each color.
3. Enlarge pattern. Draw outline on poster board.
4. Read Ephesians 6:10–17 before painting.
5. Paint full armor on poster board. Use imagination in choosing colors. Here are suggestions: waist white (truth), breastplate purple (justice),feet green (zeal), shield blue (faith), helmet orange (salvation), and sword yellow (spirit).
6. Allow to dry; the paint will crystallize as it dries.

GOD IS MY ROCK

Topic: God's Love for Us

God's love for us and his power, as our source of strength and salvation, are essential themes of scripture. In Psalm 18:3, God is described as our rock of refuge. This craft became a permanent reminder of God's love and care for our family and sits in our garden with other rocks and seashells from our vacations. The completed project may also be used as a paperweight.

What You Need

- A smooth oval-shaped rock
  (found at garden centers and creeks)
- Paintbrushes
- Acrylic paint
- Spray varnish (optional)

Steps to Follow

1. On a clean, smooth rock, paint the words "God Is My Rock." Let dry.
2. Decorate the rock with rings of color, dots, etc.
3. After drying, spray with varnish to seal, if desired.

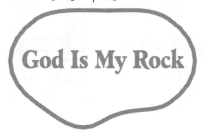

PART III—SEASONS

The Church's cycle of seasons begins each year with the First Sunday of Advent. A child's awareness of the liturgical year may be enhanced by creating memorable projects. Many of the crafts in this section are good gift ideas or may be used as part of a service project.

ADVENT DOUGH WREATH

Topic: Advent Season

Create this simple Advent wreath to mark the time of waiting for Jesus' coming. The four candles, traditionally three purple and one pink, represent the four Sundays before Christmas. The pink candle is lit on the Third Sunday of Advent (Gaudete Sunday), a joyous sign that our waiting is nearly over.

What You Need

- Wide mouth canning jar lid with a plain top
- Glue
- Small red beads (optional)
- Birthday candles (4 white, or 3 purple and 1 pink)
- Pink and purple yarn (if using white candles)
- ¼ cup dough (made from recipe below)

Dough Recipe

> 1 cup flour
> 1 cup salt
> 1 tablespoon cream of tartar
> 1 tablespoon oil
> 1 cup water
> Green food coloring

Combine all ingredients in a medium-sized saucepan. Cook over medium heat, stirring constantly, for 3–5 minutes. The dough will form a ball while cooking. Remove from heat. When cooled, knead dough until smooth. (Yields about two cups, enough for about eight wreaths)

Steps to Follow

1. Roll two "worms" of dough, each 12" long, about ³⁄₈" in diameter. Gently twist the two pieces together.
2. Apply a layer of glue around the top edge of the jar lid.
3. Lay the dough on the jar lid to form a wreath.
4. Decorate the wreath with red beads, if desired.
5. Insert the candles in the dough. If using white candles, at the base, tie purple yarn around three candles and pink around one candle.

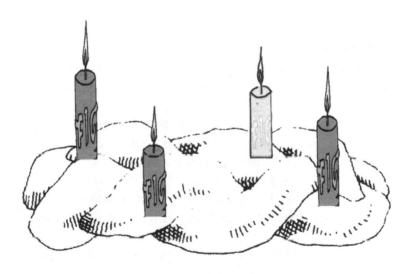

"I AM GOD'S PRECIOUS GIFT" ORNAMENT

Topic: Christmas Season

The message behind this gift is that our presence can be a gift, and that we can be Christ to others. Children will enjoy making and giving this simple ornament to friends and family.

What You Need

- Photograph of child
- Clean orange juice can lid
- Poster board
- Fine-tip markers
- Glue, Scissors, Hole-puncher
- Yarn

Steps to Follow

1. Cut the photograph into a circle 2½" in diameter.
2. Glue the photograph to the top side of the orange juice lid
3. Cut the poster board into the star shape using the pattern (enlarged) as a guide.
4. Write on the points of the star, "I am God's Precious Gift."
5. Decorate the edges of the star as desired.
6. Glue the back of the orange juice lid to the star.
7. Punch a hole at the top of the star.
8. Cut a 10" piece of yarn. Loop the yarn through the hole and tie the ends together.

JESSE TREE

Topic: Old Testament

The Jesse tree is named after Jesse, the father of David, the great king of Israel. The symbols used on the Jesse Tree represent the ancestors of Jesus from the Old Testament.

What You Need

- Medium weight sandpaper cut to 4¼" × 5½"
- Scissors
- Iron
- Construction paper in light colors
- Weighted container to hold small tree branch
- Tree branch
- Hole-puncher
- String
- Newspaper
- Crayons
- Markers or pencils

Steps to Follow

For each symbol:

1. Using crayons, color directly onto the rough side of the sandpaper. Colored surface should feel smooth when finished.
2. Preheat iron to low setting (no steam). Place construction paper on newspaper.
3. Place colored surface of sandpaper face down on construction paper.

4. Place one sheet of newspaper over sandpaper to protect iron. Using warm, dry iron, press on picture to transfer design. Carefully lift one corner to check transfer.
5. Add descriptive words for each picture after pictures have cooled. Trim any excess paper. Punch hole at top of picture and hang with string on tree branch.

Suggested Symbols

Apple—Adam and Eve
Cross—the promise of the Savior
Rainbow—Noah and ark
An altar of stones—the promise to Abraham and Sarah that they would have a son
Twelve men—the sons of Jacob and his wives, who founded the twelve tribes of Israel
Parting of the Red Sea—Moses and the Exodus
Ruth—an ancestor of Jesus
David—the king chosen by God
City—David captured Jerusalem and made it his capital
Baby—Prophets predicted the birth of an infant Savior
Bethlehem—where the Messiah was born

CHRISTMAS ALTARPIECES

Topic: Christmas Season

An altarpiece portrays a picture of a religious subject. The artwork was either painted directly on the wall or framed and hung behind the altar. Some altarpieces were set directly on the altar. (These can be found in museums today.) In the Middle Ages, altarpieces sometimes included silver and gold composition set with jewels.

What You Need

- Old Christmas cards
- Black construction paper, 12" x 18"
- Gold and silver trim
- Small fashion jewels
- Glue
- Scissors

Steps to Follow

1. Lay black construction paper flat and fold on dotted lines (as shown on facing page).
2. Cut the top to form a peak (as shown on facing page).
3. Unfold and glue card cutouts in the three main sections(as shown on facing page).
4. Decorate with gold and silver trim.
5. Glue jewels as desired.
6. Lay flat to dry. Stand up when dry.

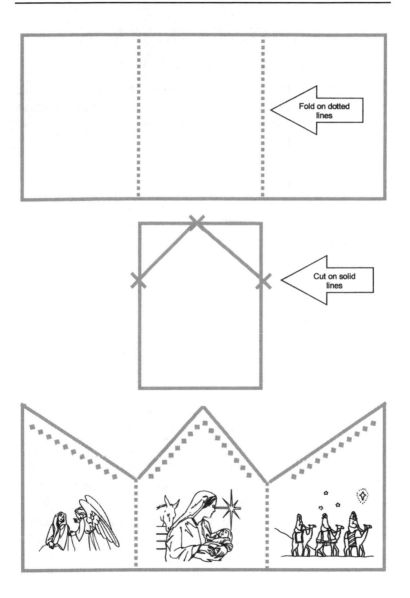

Fold on dotted lines

Cut on solid lines

HOLY FAMILY TRIARAMA

Topic: Christmas Season

During the twelve days following Christmas day, we reflect on the mystery of the Incarnation. Scripture gives us little insight into Jesus' childhood. In story, art, and song, Christians reflect on the life of the Holy Family.

What You Need

- One piece of blue construction paper
- One piece of white construction paper
- Nativity stickers
- Markers or crayons
- Foil stars
- Stapler
- Scissors

Steps to Follow

1. Cut each piece of construction paper into an 8½" square.
2. Fold each piece of paper, matching diagonal corners. When you unfold each paper, you will have an X creased in the middle of each sheet of paper.
3. On each paper cut from one corner to the center.
4. Fold the papers in the middle, so you have two triangle shapes showing. Use this space on the blue paper to apply the Nativity stickers, drawing and coloring details such as a stable. Apply the foil stars to the sky area.

5. On the white folded paper, the child can draw and color a picture of his (her) family.
6. Unfold the paper after lapping one triangle over the other using the cut edges; staple to form a standing triangle.
7. Fold the other paper the same way, and staple the two triangles together to form a triarama.

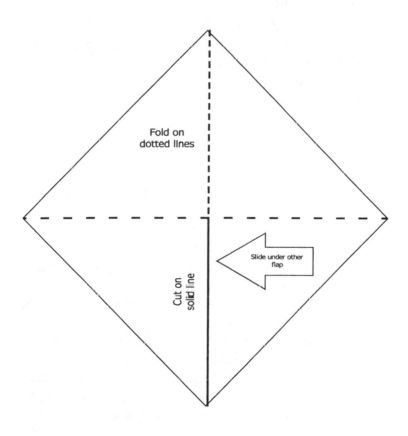

Fold on dotted lines

Slide under other flap

Cut on solid line

EPIPHANY CARD

Topic: Christmas Season

The gospel of Matthew, chapter 2, describes astrologers seeking Jesus. These Gentile wise men from the east followed a special star that marked the place of Jesus' birth.

What You Need

- One sheet of blue construction paper
- One sheet of light brown construction paper
- One sheet of dark brown construction paper
- Foil stars
- Wallpaper scraps or designed paper
- Scissors
- Glue

Steps to Follow

1. Fold the piece of blue construction paper in half to make a card.
2. Use bottom pattern (enlarged) to trace three different wise men on wallpaper scraps.
3. Use top pattern (enlarged) to trace one camel on brown paper.
4. Tear three large pieces of brown paper, two of one shade and one of the other shade.
5. Cut the brown paper pieces so that they are the same width as the front of the card.
6. Glue the brown paper pieces on the card, starting at the middle and overlapping. Use the last piece for the bottom of the card to make mountains.

7. Glue the wise men and the camel in various places on the card, with one man leading the camel.
8. Place foil stars in the blue sky.
9. Write a message on the inside of the card.

LENT TO EASTER FLOWER

Topic: Lenten Season

Plant a flower seed at the beginning of the Lenten season, care for it, and watch it grow into a beautiful flower. Lent is a time of spiritual growth, and the growing flower reminds us to nurture our relationship with God. The plant makes a nice Easter gift.

What You Need
- Potting soil
- Acrylic paints
- Paintbrushes
- Spoons
- Zinnia or Marigold seeds (use small plant variety)
- Small clay pots
- Paper and pencil

Steps to Follow
1. With paper and pencil, plan the design for your flower pot. You may work the same design around the pot, or use several symbols in a pattern. Suggested designs for Lent and Easter: a cross, a dogwood flower, an egg, or palm branches.
2. Paint the design on the outside of the flower pot.
3. Fill the inside of the clay pot with potting soil.
4. Plant a few seeds at the recommended depth.
5. Keep in a warm, well lit location. Water frequently.
6. Watch it grow!

HOT CROSS BUNS

Topic: Lenten Season

Hot Cross Buns are a food enjoyed during the season of Lent. Originally, the custom of baking these sweet rolls began in England on Good Friday. The cross icing on the top of each bun reminds us of the cross of Jesus.

What You Need

- One package of hot roll mix
- 2 Tbs melted butter
- 2 Tbs chopped raisins
- 2 Tbs mixed fruit, dried and chopped
- 1/3 cup sugar
- 1 tsp ground cinnamon
- 1 tsp ground nutmeg
- White frosting (the pre-mixed decorator tube type works well)

Steps to Follow

1. Prepare the roll mix according to package directions.
2. Add butter, raisins, chopped fruit, sugar, cinnamon, and nutmeg.
3. Cover with a towel and let rise one hour.
4. Shape into twelve buns. Place on lightly greased baking sheet. Cover and let rise 45 minutes.
5. Bake at 375° until lightly golden. Cool on wire racks.
6. Make crosses using frosting over the center of each bun.

STATIONS OF THE CROSS

Topic: Lenten Season

Illustrate and re-enact Jesus' journey to Calvary.

What You Need

- 7 Sheets of white poster board
- 14 Pre-cut brown construction paper crosses
- Glue, Markers, Crayons

Steps to Follow

1. Cut white poster board in half to make fourteen 14" x 22" pieces.
2. Give each group or child a brown paper cross, a poster board, glue and coloring supplies.
3. Assign each group a station of the cross to illustrate. The brown cross will unify the stations.
4. Encourage students to work on a large scale to fill the space so the work will be easily seen when displayed.
5. Display completed stations around room or in a hallway. Pray the stations together.

Stations of the Cross

Jesus is condemned to death.

Jesus bears his cross.

Jesus falls the first time, beneath the cross.

Jesus meets his mother.

Simon of Cyrene helps Jesus carry his cross.

Veronica wipes the face of Jesus.

Jesus falls the second time.

Jesus comforts the women of Jerusalem.

Jesus falls the third time.

Jesus is stripped of his clothes and given gall to drink.

Jesus is nailed to the cross.

Jesus dies on the cross.

Jesus is taken down from the cross and laid in Mary's arms.

Jesus is buried in the tomb.

EASTER LILY CARD

Topic: Easter Season

The lily is a sign of joy at Easter, the resurrection, and the promise of eternal life. Many churches decorate the altar with lilies at Eastertime.

What You Need

- Sheet of black construction paper
- Green and yellow construction paper
- Silver paint pen
- White tissue paper, about 4" x 4"

Steps to Follow

1. Fold black construction paper in half (width of paper)
2. Trace flower pattern on front side of card.
3. Using scissors, carefully cut out flower shape beginning at "x" and cutting on pattern edge, leaving flower shape opening upon completion. Discard flower cutout.
4. Cover opening with white tissue paper. Glue to inside of card, applying glue to the edges of the tissue paper only.
5. Use green scraps to cut leaves and a stem for the flower. Glue to front of card under the flower.

6. Cut a pistil for center of flower from yellow paper. Carefully attach to center of tissue paper lily.
7. Using the silver paint pen, write a greeting on inside and outside of card.

PART IV—SAINTS

The stories of the lives of the saints enrich our Christian heritage. The saints' faith and courage are models for children to live out their beliefs. Several of the crafts in this section are adaptable to any favorite saint. Use the projects throughout the year: on saints' feast days, baptism anniversaries, birthdays, and at times when the Church honors Mary.

HOLY CARD MAGNETS

Topic: All Saints' Day

The stories of the lives of the saints can remind us how to live our faith in God daily. Read about the saints and make these magnets to remind you daily to follow Jesus.

What You Need

- A variety of cards
- Rubber cement and glue
- Magnetic sheets with adhesive backing
- Black or dark-colored poster board
- Assorted trims, beads, and buttons

Steps to Follow

1. Pre-cut poster board to a half-inch larger on each side than the holy card.
2. Cut magnetic sheets to the size of the pre-cut poster board.
3. Peel adhesive backing protector from magnetic sheets and adhere to the poster board.
4. Using rubber cement, glue the holy card to the center of the poster board.
5. Decorate around the edges of the holy card, using glue and trims.

Extension Activity

Take photographs of children dressed up as their favorite saint. Mount the picture on poster board and complete as directed above.

STICK PUPPET SAINT

Topic: All Saints' Day, celebrating saints' feast days

The Church honors saints on their feast days and on All Saints' Day. We retell the stories of the lives of the saints to keep them alive in our memory and to learn from their lives. Use the puppet pattern as a basis for many different saint puppets. The puppets can be used as props in student produced plays on the saints' lives.

What You Need

- Heavy weight, solid colored fabric scraps (burlap, denim, canvas) about 8" x 5"
- Paint stirring stick
- Scissors
- Popsicle stick
- 2-inch circle of tan or yellow paper
- Glue or glue gun
- String, about 6" long
- Personalizing materials, if desired

Steps to Follow

1. Attach the popsicle stick at a right angle to the paint stirrer about 3" down from the top, centered.
2. Fold the fabric in half lengthwise, cutting a hole in the folded edge just large enough to insert the paint stirrer.
3. Trim away excess fabric as shown by the colored boxes to create a garment.

4. Draw a face on the circle of paper and attach to the top of the paint stirrer.
5. Use the string to tie the garment closed.
6. Add any personalizing details such as a small bag for St. Nicholas, a crown with candles for St. Lucia, a green shamrock and crozier for St. Patrick, or animals for St. Francis.

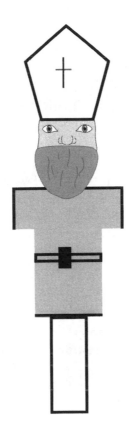

OUR LADY OF GUADALUPE MOSAIC

Topic: Mary, Our Lady of Guadalupe

Mary appeared to Juan Diego in Mexico at Mount Tepeyac in 1531. Mary promised to show pity and compassion for all who trusted in God. This mosaic represents the image of Our Lady of Guadalupe.

What You Need

- Poster board cut to 8½" x 11"
- Glue, Scissors
- Old Magazines
- Fine-tip, black permanent marker
- Flower stickers

Steps to Follow

1. Enlarge pattern to fit an 8½" x 11" sheet of paper.
2. Tear or cut colors from old magazines into small squares. These will be used to fill in the various areas of the image.
3. Glue image to the cut piece of poster board.
4. Glue colored squares to create a colorful mosaic of Our Lady of Guadalupe.
5. Draw facial features with a fine-tip, black permanent marker.
6. Use sticker flowers as a border to complete project.

LIFE OF MARY BANNER

Topic: Mary

Mary, the mother of Jesus, is a model of discipleship. Create this banner to learn about Mary's life. October and May are traditional months to honor Mary. Up to seven children may create one banner. Depending on your group's size, you may create several banners.

What You Need

- Felt, burlap or paper 7" x 15"
- Yarn
- Craft glue
- Variety of colored markers
- Colored pencils
- White drawing paper

Steps to Follow

1. Assign each student a time of Mary's life to illustrate from this sequence of events:

   Luke 1:26–38   God sent the angel Gabriel to a virgin named Mary in Nazareth.

   Luke 1:39–45   Mary visits Elizabeth.

   Luke 2:4–7   Jesus is born.

   Luke 2:41–52   Mary and Joseph find Jesus at the Temple.

   John 2:1–11   Wedding at Cana in Galilee.

   John 19:25–27   Mary at the foot of Jesus' cross. Mary's assumption into heaven.

2. Distribute white drawing paper, markers, and colored pencils. Have each child label their paper with the title of their illustration. Encourage the children to fill the paper with their drawing.

3. Compile the seven drawings in chronological order. Depending on your hanging space, make the banner horizontal or vertical. Bead glue around the edges of drawing paper and lay on banner to dry. Hot glue works well, if applied by an adult.

4. If making a vertical banner, fold 3 inches on top edge and glue or staple in place. Insert dowel in the fold. Tightly wrap yarn around the ends of dowel, leaving enough slack to hang banner. If making a horizontal banner, attach to wall or bulletin board.

PATRON SAINT PLACEMAT

Topic: All Saints' Day/Patron Saint Feast Day

Create this placemat as a reminder of the life story of a favorite saint. Using story and symbol, highlight what you like and treasure about your special saint.

What You Need

- 12" x 18" drawing paper
- Crayons or markers
- Ruler
- Clear contact paper, enough to cover both sides of the placemat
- Construction paper
- Glue
- Stickers

Steps to Follow

1. On the drawing paper, color a picture of your favorite saint. Write about his or her life.
2. For the border, use stickers (shamrocks for St. Patrick, candy canes for St. Nicholas, books and schoolhouses for Elizabeth Ann Seton, animals and birds for St. Francis of Assisi) to decorate.
3. Cut two pieces of contact paper slightly larger than 12" x 18" placemat.
4. Allow the glue to dry, and then apply the contact paper to the placemat.
5. Trim any excess edges of contact paper.

PUPPET THEATER
(AND MORE PUPPET IDEAS)

Topic: All Saints' Day

Children will enjoy telling the stories of saints' lives and other events in the history of the Church using this easy-to-make puppet theater.

What You Need

- A six-foot length of heavy weight, tightly woven fabric such as denim or twill, 48"–54" wide
- Thread
- Two wooden dowel rods 36" long
- Spring tension rod approx. 50" long
- Trim (optional)

Steps to Follow

1. Trim the selvages off the sides of the fabric piece. Hem the side edges narrowly.
2. Hem the bottom. Fold the top over making a 1' pocket. Sew across the hem.
3. From the top of the piece, measure down 12". Cut a rectangular opening in the fabric 24" by 32".
4. Clip the corners of the opening 1 inch diagonally. Fold the edges of the opening to the inside and hem, leaving the ends open of each side. Insert the dowels into the rod pockets of the top and bottom opening.

5. If you wish, decorate the theater with fabric paint, trim, or add a removable curtain over the opening.
6. Insert the spring tension rod into the top opening. Hang the theater by mounting the rod the frame of a doorway.

Finger puppets

Finger puppets are small and can best be used individually or in small groups. Finger puppets can be made several ways. Cut small bands of paper to fit around the finger, then mount decorated paper faces to the band. Or, cut bands from felt and sew together. Children may decorate the puppets to make animals or people.

Hand puppets

Hand puppets are easily made from felt or paper lunch bags or socks. To make a felt hand puppet, trace an outline of a hand, cut shape from felt and sew together. Let the children decorate with yarn, fabric scraps, buttons, and other trim.

Clothespin puppets

Old fashioned wooden nonspring clothespins, paint or markers, felt, trim, and cloth scraps are the materials you will need. The top of the clothespin is the puppet's head and the pin is the body. Clothe and decorate as desired.

Spoon puppets

Using the back of a wooden or plastic spoon as the face, decorate with markers, paint, yarn for hair, and hats. Cut out clothes and glue to handle to make the body of the puppet.

PART V—PRAYERS

Both formal and informal prayers help us to deepen our relationship with God. The project ideas in this section can serve as reminders of the importance of prayer in our lives. Craft ideas in other sections of this book can also be used for the topic of prayer, such as the painted votive candle and the holy water font. Create these projects to encourage children to pray.

THE ROSARY

Topic: Honoring Mary

We honor Mary when praying the rosary and remember the important events of her life while meditating on the Joyful, Sorrowful, and Glorious Mysteries. With the finished rosary, pray a decade together to demonstrate the sequence of prayers.

What You Need

- Nylon bead-stringing thread
- Clear nail polish
- 53 beads of one color (color A)
- 6 beads of a second color (color B)
- 14 small, clear beads for spacers
- A cross and medal cut from project board, using the diagram as a model. (These may be colored, if desired.)
- Scissors

Steps to Follow

1. Cut a length of thread, about a yard long. Seal one end with nail polish.
2. Tie the cross to the unsealed end of the thread.
3. Begin threading the beads. Start with a clear bead, followed by one of color B; then a clear bead, next three of color A, next a clear, then one of color B, followed by another clear bead.
4. Thread the medal onto the rosary as shown in the center piece detail diagram.

5. String on one clear bead, ten beads of color A, one clear bead, one bead of color B.
6. Repeat step 5 three times.
7. For the last decade, thread one clear bead, ten beads of color A, and one clear bead.
8. Using the center piece diagram, thread the medal as shown. Tie a knot to secure the rosary.
9. Seal both knots with nail polish.

PERSONAL GOD BOX

Topic: Prayer, Faith

Our faith journey begins at baptism and continues throughout our lives. A "God Box" is a place to store treasured mementos, cards, photos, rosaries, medals, and stories of your personal faith journey.

What You Need

- Cigar box or other small paper box with lid
- Decorative gift wrap
- Old magazines
- Beads, jewels, and trim
- Glue
- Scissors
- Modge podge
- Paintbrushes
- Newspaper

Steps to Follow

1. Cover the outside and inside of the box and lid with paper, using either gift wrap or collage style with cutouts from magazines.
2. After papering, paint a thin layer of modge podge over papered surfaces.
3. Glue on beads and trim.

PRAYER PAL

Topic: Prayer

Mother Teresa said: "Try to feel the need for prayer often during the day and take the trouble to pray. Prayer makes the heart large enough until it can contain God's gift of Himself. Ask and seek, and your heart will grow big enough to receive Him and keep Him as your own."

What You Need

- Colorful sheets of thin fun foam
- Colorful small shapes of fun foam (pre-cut and sold in bags)
- Glitter glue
- Narrow grosgrain ribbon
- Copies of butterfly pattern (or use cookie cutter or die cut machine if available)
- Copy of prayer for each child
- Contact paper
- Scissors, hole puncher
- Index card (optional)

Steps to Follow

1. Reproduce a copy of a prayer. As an option, create your own prayer on an index card. Cover prayer card with clear contact paper. Punch a hole in a corner of prayer card.
2. Reproduce butterfly pattern for students to trace. Or, use cookie cutters to trace pattern, or use pre-cut shapes from die cut machine.

3. Cut butterfly from fun foam. Punch a hole in butterfly.
4. Decorate the butterfly with shapes of fun foam and glitter glue.
5. Allow glue to dry.
6. Attach prayer to butterfly with ribbon.
7. Place the prayer pal near your bed or in your backpack as a reminder to pray often.

GUARDIAN ANGEL

Topic: Prayer

The Guardian Angel prayer is a simple prayer many children learn at an early age:

> Angel of God, my guardian dear,
> To whom God's love commits me here.
> Ever this day (night) be at my side
> To light and guard,
> To rule and guide. Amen.

What You Need

- Thin, fluted edged 9" paper plates
- Glue, stapler
- Scissors, tape
- Colored pencils
- **Optional:** gold spray paint, gold pipe cleaner, braid or tinsel garland for halo cut 1½" long. Stickers, glitter, ribbons, or stars to decorate skirt.

Steps to Follow

1. Transfer the pattern (enlarged to fit paper plate) to the paper plate. The outline edge is given only as a guide. Do not transfer.
2. Transfer the left and right wing patterns to another paper plate. The pattern shows you where to place the edge of the wing so that the scallops of the plate become the ruffles on the edge of the angel's wings.)

3. Cut on the line starting from the edge of the paper plate up to the head. Cut out small rectangles in the head area, as they form the bottom of the angel's hair. Do not cut the dotted lines; these are fold marks.

4. To shape the plate into the angel, turn the plate over so the edge curves to the inside and all the pencil marks are to the backside. Hold the two skirt edges where you cut the slit and overlap about 6 inches.

5. Pull the hands and head forward slightly. Bend the arms away from the body. Bend them again at the elbow.

6. Cut a 1-inch slit in each of the grooves of the wings. Gently shape the paper wings so they roll away from the angel's body. Staple the wings in place, one on top of the other, onto the back of the angel's skirt.

7. Using colored pencils, decorate angel, and attach a halo to the head with the gold trim.

8. If desired, attach a copy of the Guardian Angel prayer to the angel.

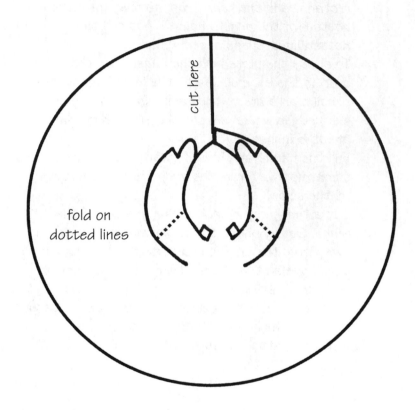

cut here

fold on
dotted lines

center design on
paper plate

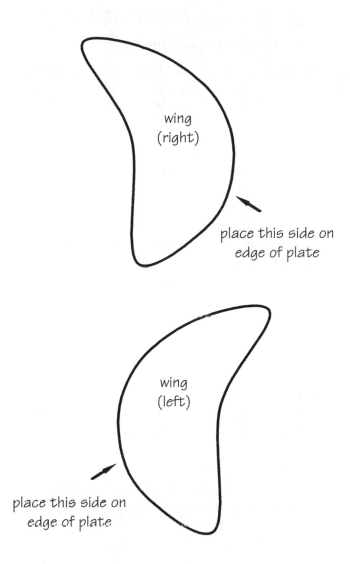

wing
(right)

place this side on
edge of plate

wing
(left)

place this side on
edge of plate

SPIRITUAL BOUQUET

Topic: Prayer Offering

A spiritual bouquet is a traditional prayer offering. Children may create this card for an anniversary, Mother's Day, Father's Day, or birthday gift.

What You Need

- 11" × 17" yellow construction paper (one per two students)
- 8½" × 11" black construction paper (one per two students)
- Large assortment of various geometric shapes cut from brightly colored paper
- Large scraps of green construction paper
- Scissors, glue
- Fine-tip black marker or pen

Steps to Follow

1. Cut black construction paper to 4" × 11". Cut yellow construction paper to 5½" × 13".
2. Cut curving stem shapes from the green paper to form stem pieces, about ½" wide.
3. Glue green strips to the black sheet, making sure both ends of the strips are touching different edges of the black sheet (see diagram). Uses 3–5 strips. These will be the stems of the flowers.
4. Use the assortment of geometric shapes (slightly enlarged) to make flowers.

Imaginary flowers are acceptable.

5. Cut large leaf shapes using the pattern (enlarged, if desired) provided. Add to stems in empty spaces.

6. On large flower petals, write the name and number of prayers being offered for the recipient of this Spiritual Bouquet.

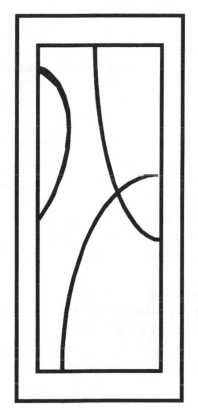

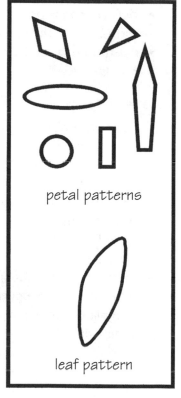

petal patterns

leaf pattern

example of stem

CRAYON RESIST CREED

Topic: Prayer, Faith

In the Nicene Creed we profess our basic beliefs. In this bulletin board display, each child expresses in art a part of the creed.

What You Need

- Bulletin board paper
- Permanent black marker, crayons
- Blue tempera paint with water added to make a wash
- Sponge brush

Steps to Follow

1. Tear off a piece of paper, large enough to cover bulletin board. If desired, draw an outline of a church on the outer edges of the paper.
2. Using the marker, divide the paper into 20 boxes. (Four rows of five works well.)
3. With the marker, write one section of the Nicene Creed in each box. Suggestions are given on the next page.
4. Using crayons, illustrate the text in each box.
5. When complete, cover the entire sheet with the diluted blue paint to create a crayon resist effect.

Suggestions for Step 3:

We believe in one God, the Father Almighty, maker of heaven and earth,/

of all that is seen and unseen./

We believe in one Lord, Jesus Christ, the only Son of God,/

eternally begotten of the Father,/

God from God, Light from Light, true God from true God,/

begotten, not made, one in Being with the Father./

Through him all things were made./

For us men and for our salvation he came down from heaven:/

By the power of the Holy Spirit he was born of the Virgin Mary, and became man./

For our sake he was crucified under Pontius Pilate;/

He suffered, died and was buried./

On the third day he rose again in fulfillment of the Scriptures;/

He ascended into heaven and is seated at the right hand of the Father./

He will come again in glory to judge the living and the dead, and his kingdom will have no end./

We believe in the Holy Spirit, the Lord the giver of life, Who proceeds from the Father and the Son./

With the Father and the Son he is worshiped and glorified /

He has spoken through the Prophets./

We believe in one holy catholic and apostolic Church./

We acknowledge one baptism for the forgiveness of sins./

We look for the resurrection of the dead, and the life of the world to come. Amen.

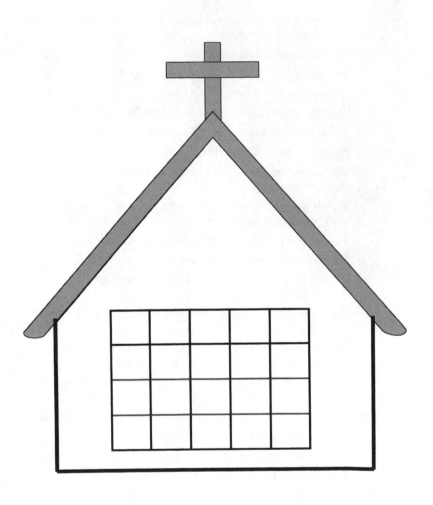

PRAYING HANDS

Topic: Prayer, Faith

In prayer we build a relationship with God. Children may adapt this craft to any of the traditional prayers or create their own prayer.

What You Need

- Light colored construction paper
- Pencil
- Scissors
- Stickers, markers
- Copies of traditional prayers
  (Our Father, Hail Mary, Act of Contrition, etc.)

Steps to Follow

1. Fold construction paper in half, 8½" sides together.
2. Place hand flat on paper, fingers together, with little finger on folded edge of paper.
3. Trace around hand.
4. Cut out hand shape, except along the folded edge.
5. Unfold praying hands. Write the prayer on the inside. (Copies of prayer may be substituted.)
6. Decorate as desired and display.